This book belongs to:

____

____

____

Lucia was a very cheerful and happy girl who had lots of friends. At school, she was good at maths and science.

Lucia enjoyed playing with plasticine, Lego, toy cars and Scalextric. She was good at football and liked to keep healthy and strong.

SCHOOL

At home, Lucia always helped her Mum with jobs that needed to be done which made her Mum very happy!

Sometimes, Lucia even helped her
Dad to fix broken things in the garage and
garden.

Lucia was always willing and happy to help
with a big smile on her face as she was doing
jobs; she never grumbled.

As Lucia got older, she had to decide what she wanted to do as a career. She thought back to her favourite subjects at school and all the things she loved to do.

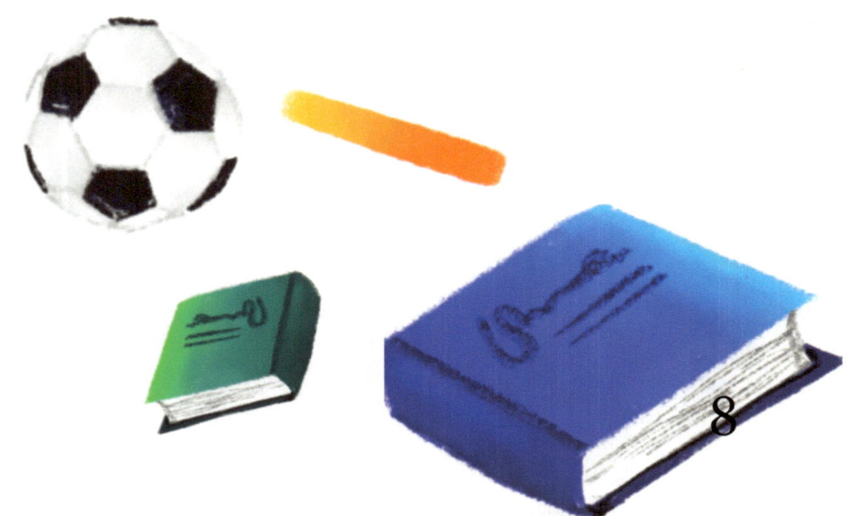

9

Lucia had a friend called Micah who had
always wanted to become an electrician.
He had talked about it a lot and it sounded like
it would be very interesting!

11

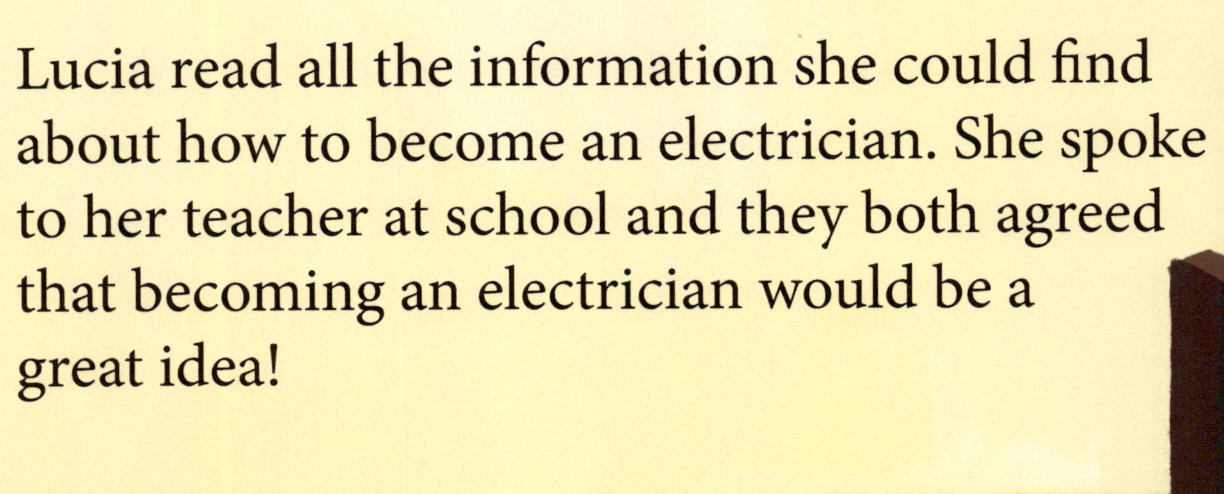

Lucia read all the information she could find about how to become an electrician. She spoke to her teacher at school and they both agreed that becoming an electrician would be a great idea!

After she finished secondary school, Lucia went to college and took an apprenticeship to become an electrician.

She went to college for two days a week and she worked on a building site for three days a week where she learnt so much!

Lucia had to use so many tools and at first she did not know what they all did but she quickly learnt their names and their functions. She soon started using the tools very well!

At the end of her time at college, Lucia had to take a written exam and a practical exam to show how much she had learnt. Her family and friends encouraged her and said that she would be a very good electrician.

When it was time for her to take the written and practical exams, she was very nervous. The examiner was kind and advised her not to worry, she was sure that Lucia would do well!

19

All the had work paid off and Lucia passed all of her exams! She was very, very happy. All of her family and friends were so proud and they had a party to celebrate her success!

There were some challenges at work and being an electrician was sometimes very tiring.

Lucia still played football with her friends and helped her Mum and Dad around the house.

As she had learnt so much, Lucia could even help her neighbours and her friends; it made her happy to know that people really appreciated the work she did.

23

Once Lucia became qualified, she was able to look for good jobs as an electrician. Some jobs required her to travel around the country but she didn't mind because she made new friends wherever she went!

LUCIA THE
ELECTRICIAN

Lucia was very happy because she had achieved her goal of becoming an excellent electrician! It all started from when she was a little girl because had lots of ambition and direction.

It took time for Lucia to learn how to become an excellent electrician, but she did what was needed. Lots of employers wanted to have her as part of their team because she always did a very good job in her work.

If you want to become an excellent electrician you can, just like Lucia!

If you want to be an excellent electrician, look at these references to learn how!

Fun Kids Live
An interactive website introducing children to the job of an electrician. Good to engage children aged 6-12 with the world of energy.
www.funkidslive.com/learn/energyexplained/episode-10-jobs/

The School Run
Basic introduction to electricity for school children aged 9+
www.theschoolrun.com/what-is-electricity

Ducksters
Basic introduction to the science behind electricity for children aged 7+
www.ducksters.com/science/electricity_101.php

BBC Bitesize
BBC bitesize intro to electricity for Key Stage 2 children
https://www.bbc.co.uk/bitesize/topics/zj44jxs

<u>**For parents and guardians:**</u>

National Careers
National careers service summary of essential aspects of being an electrician.
www.nationalcareers.service.gov.uk/job-profiles/electrician

Trade Skills 4 U
Guidance on how to become an electrician in 4 steps from domestic electrical installer to NVQ level 3
www.tradeskills4u.co.uk/pages/become-an-electrician

UCAS
Universities and Colleges Admissions Service (UCAS) guidance on the role of an electrician and the training required to become qualified.
www.ucas.com/ucas/after-gcses/find-career-ideas/explore-jobs/job-profile/electrician

What do you want to be when you grow up? Draw it below!

Notes!

Check out some other books in the series!

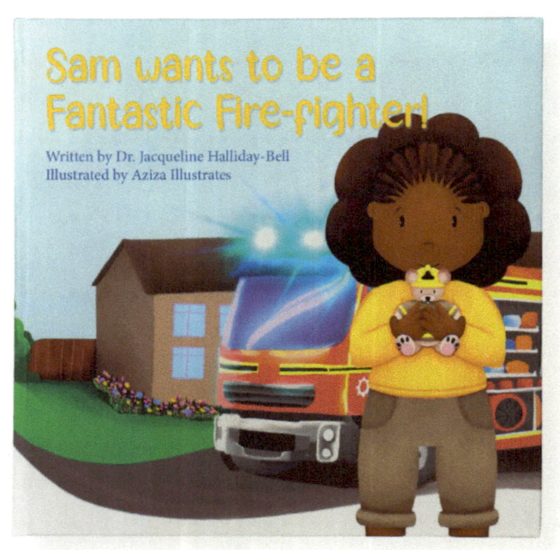

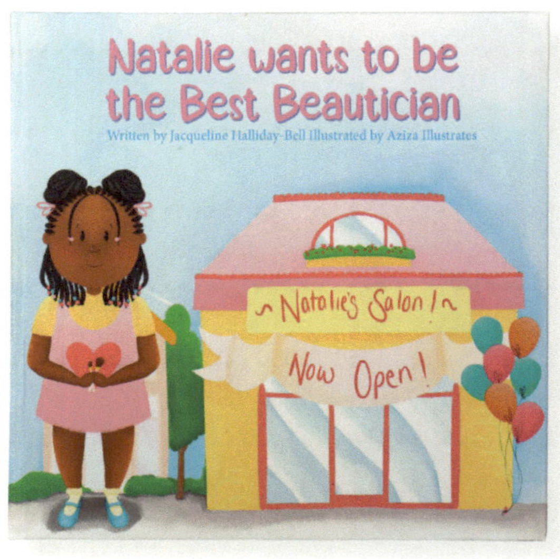